Jonathan Edwards on Movements

DAVE COLES

Pastor's Edition

Copyright © 2023 by Dave Coles

All rights reserved. No part of this publication may be reproduced, stored in a retrieval system, or transmitted in any form by any means, electronic, mechanical, photocopy, recording, or otherwise, without the prior permission of the publisher, except as provided for by USA copyright law.

Published by Beyond
301 S. Sherman St.
Richardson, TX

Pastor's edition ISBN: 979-8-9870207-2-2

All quotations from *The Works of Jonathan Edwards, Volumes 1 and 2* are used by permission of Banner of Truth Trust.

Dear Pastor,

Thank you for your ministry of God's word to your community and for your passion to make Jesus known – locally and throughout the world.

Recent days have seen considerable discussion on the topic of movements to Christ being reported widely across the world. Whenever I hear of something new or different purporting to bring great Kingdom fruit, I like to consider how it fits (or not) with the wisdom of giants of the faith who have gone before us.

Ever since my earliest years as a pastor, I have often found great wisdom and insight when I turn to the writings of Jonathan Edwards, that clarion voice from New England, who still has much to say to us today across three centuries. Many have forgotten that Edwards' preaching ministry took place in the midst of the dynamic, yet controversial, Great Awakening. So, it's no surprise that Jonathan Edwards had much to say about movements.

With this in mind, I thought it might be of interest to you to revisit "Jonathan Edwards on Movements," to receive from him the light he shared in the midst of all the heat of movements occurring around him. I trust that this resource will be as helpful to your church as it has been to many others— whether they work with Beyond or others who labor to see God's Kingdom fill the whole earth.

God bless you as you continue to serve Christ in your community.

Sincerely,
Dave Coles
Editor, *Jonathan Edwards on Movements*

Table of Contents

Introduction	vii
1. Signs which Should Not be Considered Evidence that a Work is Not from the Spirit of God	1
2. Distinguishing Scripture Evidences of a Work of the Spirit of God	17
3. Practical Inferences	25
4. Additional Insights from "Thoughts on the Revival"	49
Conclusion	61
Books Cited	63

Introduction

The world was a very different place nearly 300 years ago, when Jonathan Edwards wrote about events taking place during what we know as the First Great Awakening. He wrote in the context of Massachusetts Bay Colony, a British outpost of Protestant Christendom inhabited by Puritans, all professing Christians. In his essays that I will cite, Edwards responded to criticisms of that awakening with careful, biblically-based analysis of pros and cons of the events taking place.

Though current discussions about Church Planting Movements and Disciple Making Movements[1] are hap-

---

[1] Stan Parks and Dave Coles define a Church Planting Movement as: "(result): a multiplication of disciples making disciples, and leaders developing leaders, resulting in indigenous churches (usually house churches) planting more churches. These new disciples and churches begin spreading rapidly through a people group or population segment, [with] consistent, multiple-stream 4th generation reproduction of churches," and Disciple Making Movement as "a process toward a Church Planting Movement." *24:14 – A Testimony to All Peoples (Spring, Texas: 24:14, 2019)* 315.

This essay does *not* attempt to address issues related to Insider Movements (see for example "Insider Movements: Current Issues in Discussion," by L.D. Waterman in *Evangelical Review of Theology,* October 2013 (37:4, 292-307)) or the Church Growth Movement, phenomena distinct from Church Planting Movements. This also does not include evangelism movements or people movements, in which converts are often not well discipled.

vii

pening primarily among *unreached* people groups in Asia and Africa, and thus employ many terms not found in Edwards' writings, still the Lord has not changed, the Bible has not changed, and the gospel has not changed. Accordingly, Edwards' incisive and edifying analysis offers numerous insights that endure through the centuries. For this reason, we can still discern in Edwards' insights on the various spiritual phenomena of his day, principles that apply to subsequent revivals and movements of the Spirit even for our day.

In one sense, any attempt to directly apply Edwards' words to present-day concerns involves inherent anachronisms. Yet drawing on perspectives and biblically-based analyses from a spiritual giant of the past can greatly increase our wisdom in the present. Any insights we can glean from Edwards' comments on the Awakening can shed light on current thoughts and discussions about movements taking place in our time.

Edwards' essay "The Distinguishing Marks of a Work of the Spirit of God" expounds on 1 John 4:1 ("*Beloved, believe not every spirit, but try the spirits whether they are of God; because many false prophets are gone out into the world*") and consists of three sections:

Most Church Planting Movements and Disciple Making Movements share great concern for healthy (biblical) disciples leading to healthy (biblical) churches. See, for example, "What is Church? From Surveying Scripture to Applying in Culture," by L.D. Waterman, *EMQ*, October 2011.

1. "NEGATIVE SIGNS *or, What are no signs by which we are to judge of a work and especially, What are no evidences that a work is not from the Spirit of God*" (*Marks*, 261).
2. "*What are distinguishing scripture evidences of a work of the Spirit of God*" (*Marks*, 266).
3. "*Practical inferences*" (*Marks*, 269).

I will follow this broad outline, interspersing quotations from other works of Edwards along the way, then adding additional insights from Edwards' "Thoughts on the Revival" which don't fit within the outline of "Distinguishing Marks."

1

Signs Which Should Not be Considered Evidence that a Work is Not from the Spirit of God

Edwards elucidates nine factors (signs) which should *not* be used to judge whether or not something is from the Spirit of God.[2] Four of the nine (physical effects, strong affections for God, example as a great means, and ter-

---
[2] These negative signs are:
1. Newness. "If a work is carried on in a very unusual and extraordinary way" (Marks, 261).
2. Physical Effects. "A work is not to be judged by any effects on the bodies of men" (Marks, 261).
3. Strong Affections for God. "They are very much moved" (Marks, 262).
4. Impressions on the Imagination. "Many...have great impressions made on their imaginations" (Marks, 262).
5. Example is a Great Means of it. "They are influenced by example" (Marks, 263).
6. Imprudence. "many...are guilty of great imprudence and irregularities in their conduct" (Marks, 264).
7. Errors. "many errors in judgment and some delusions of Satan that have intermixed with the work" (Marks, 265).
8. False believers. "If some...fall away into gross errors or scandalous practices" (Marks, 265).
9. Terrifying Preaching. "It seems to be promoted by ministers who insist on the terrors of God's holy Law" (Marks, 265).

rifying preaching) have not, to my knowledge, ever been mentioned as concerns or *problems* related to today's Church Planting Movements. Five of the nine, however, seem to have relevance to the current discussion of movements, since similar concerns or fears of such concerns have been (or could be) raised in critiquing movements. These factors are *newness, imprudences, impressions on the imagination, errors*, and *false believers*. Edwards describes some of these factors in much stronger terms than those used in most accusations against movements. But if his principle applies to a very blatant problem, it seems reasonable to apply it to a less glaring form (or fear) of such a problem as well.

The first such sign Edwards describes is that a phenomenon seems **new and unusual** – very different from the way we have seen the Lord normally work, or the ways he has commonly worked in the past.

> Nothing can be certainly concluded from this, That a work is carried on in a way very unusual and extraordinary; provided the variety or difference be such, as may still be comprehended within the limits of scripture rules. What the church has been used to, is not a rule by which we are to judge; because there may be new and extraordinary works of God, and he has heretofore evidently wrought in an extraordinary manner. He has brought to pass new things, strange works; and has wrought in such a manner as to surprise both men and angels. And as God has done thus in times past, so we have no reason to think

> but that he will do so still. The prophecies of Scripture give us reason to think that God has things to accomplish, which have never yet been seen. No deviation from what has hitherto been usual, let it be never so great, is an argument that a work is not from the Spirit of God, if it be no deviation from his prescribed rule. The Holy Spirit is sovereign in his operation; and we know that he uses a great variety; and we cannot tell how great a variety he may use, within the compass of the rules he himself has fixed. We ought not to limit God where he has not limited himself (*Marks*, 261).

Edwards also expounds this theme in his "Thoughts on the Revival." There, Section II elucidates the principle that, "We should judge by the rule of scripture" (*Thoughts*, 367). Rather than viewing this primarily as a limiting factor (as some have done)[3] Edwards chides those who limit God, where he has not limited himself.

> It is a great fault in us to limit a sovereign all-wise God, whose judgments are a great deep, and his ways past finding out, where he has

---

[3] Chad Vegas and Alex Kocman: "Methods are not a matter of liberty but fall under the express prescriptions of Scripture. At root, this thesis is simply an application of what theologians have named the regulative principle to the church's missionary task. In the context of public worship, the regulative principle is that Scripture's teachings, explicit and implicit, regulate church practice. *Missions by the Book: How Theology and Missions Walk Together.* (Cape Coral, FL: Founders Press, 2021), 15.

not limited himself, and in things concerning which he has not told us what his way shall be (*Thoughts,* 369).

Another thing that some make their rule to judge of this work by, instead of the Holy Scriptures, is *history,* or former observation. Herein they err two ways:

First, if there be any thing extraordinary in the circumstances of this work which was not observed in former times, theirs is a rule to reject this work... and... limit God, where he has not limited himself. And this is especially unreasonable in this case: for whosoever has well weighed the wonderful and mysterious methods of divine wisdom, in carrying on the work of the new creation – or in the progress of the work of redemption, from the first promise of the seed of the woman to this time – may easily observe that it has all along been God's manner to open new scenes, and to bring forth to view things new and wonderful – such as eye had not seen, nor ear heard, nor entered into the heart of man or angels – to the astonishment of heaven and earth, not only in the revelations he makes of his mind and will, but also in the works of his hands (*Thoughts,* 369).

Some have objected to Church Planting Movements on the grounds that some elements (such as rapid growth and newness) have similarities to positive values in Western culture.[4] Others have objected on the grounds that these movements employ some means of ministry not explicitly commanded or modeled in Scripture.[5] This comment of Edwards may have some relevance:

> It is no valid objection against examples being so much used, that the Scripture speaks of the word as the principal means of carrying on God's work; for the word of God is the principal means, nevertheless, by which other means operate and are made effectual (*Marks*, 264).

---

[4] As in Jackson Wu: "I will briefly list a few prominent features of CPM [Church Planting Movement] theory that also characterized Western cultures. The approach is distinctly focused on rapidity, numerical growth, novelty (new believers, new churches) and independence (not letting tradition encumber progress)." ("The Influence of Culture on the Evolution of Mission Methods: Using 'Church Planting Movements' as a Case Study," in *Global Missiology*, October 2014.)

[5] Vegas and Kocman: "We often hear that Scripture does not necessitate any one particular method in ministry, that matters of methodology are neutral. If the method 'works—by bringing about conversions or at least interested seekers who consider themselves obedient followers—then the method is considered to be ordained by God. These 'new measures' are christened a fresh wind of the Holy Spirit, even if their practice lacks biblical support." While the authors level this accusation against Church Planting Movements among unreached people groups, the example they cite comes from "pragmatism in the North American church growth movement" (op. cit., 13-14).

This comment from "Religious Affections" speaks even more directly to the issue:

> It is to be feared that some have gone too far towards directing the Spirit of the Lord, and marking out his footsteps for him, and limiting him to certain steps and methods. Experience plainly shows that God's Spirit is unsearchable and untraceable, in some of the best Christians, as to the method of his operation in their conversion (*Affections*, 254).

Sam Storms summarizes the point from "Religious Affections":

> The way in which people come to have their affections awakened prove nothing about whether those affections are of God or of the flesh. Many think that the only authentic affections of the heart are those that are awakened in us by the diligent use of those means appointed in Scripture. In other words, they are suspicious of people who testify to deep and profound affections of the heart without being able to account by scriptural means for how they came by them. If people cannot explain rationally how they employed their reason and the means of grace as set forth in Scripture, some judge their alleged affections as false (*Storms*, 63-64).

Storms continues his summary of Edwards' view: "The Spirit's work is mysterious and varied and subject only to the sovereign pleasure of his own will. What we must be concerned with is the nature of what God has produced in the soul and not the Spirit's method of producing it" (Storms, 68).

In discussions of modern movements, some have overly focused on one method or another, as if they knew the Lord's only method of bringing significant fruit. Others, meanwhile, have argued against use of *any* methods not explicitly mentioned in Scripture.[6] Yet others have criticized as "pragmatism"[7] any observation of what

---

[6] As noted above. Also "We cannot have confidence in any ministry unless it is specifically.... prescribed by the Scriptures, no matter how noble that ministry may be; if it's not prescribed by the Scriptures, we're in trouble." (Paul Washer, quoted favorably in *Missions by the Book*, 27.)

[7] See, for example, "Pragmatism, Pragmatism Everywhere!" by Andy Johnson, 2010. https://www.9marks.org/article/pragmatism-pragmatism-everywhere;

Also Wu, op. cit.: "The strong emphasis on 'best practices' displays a bent towards western pragmatism."

And Zane Pratt: "I sort of fear it's classic North American pragmatism." ("Are Explosive Disciple-Making Movements Really Healthy?" https://missionspodcast.com/podcast/zane-pratt-are-explosive-disciple-making-movements-really-healthy. July 2, 2018.)

Again, Wu: "Second, people can uncritically use weak (e.g. overly pragmatic) methodologies under the guise of biblical authority. If CPMs are in the Bible and CPMs are assessed according to annual percentage of growth, then it will not be long before pragmatism sets it. Practitioners will use whatever method promises the fastest result." ("There are no Church Planting Movements in the Bible: Why Biblical Exegesis and Missiological Methods cannot be Separated" *Global Missiology*, October 2014.)

bears more or less fruit, with subsequent preference for approaches that tend to bear more fruit. Edwards maintains, time and again, the folly of limiting God in his use of methods, since Scripture focuses much more on the fruit brought forth in people's lives.

> God has appeared far from limiting himself to *any certain method* in his proceedings with sinners under legal convictions (*Narrative*, 352).
>
> I have abundantly insisted, that a manifestation of sincerity in *fruits brought forth,* is better than any manifestation they can make of it [conversion] in *words* alone (*Narrative*, 355).
>
> There is an endless *variety* in the particular manner and circumstances in which persons are wrought on; and an opportunity of seeing so much will show, that God is further from confining himself to a particular method in his work on souls, than some imagine.... The work of God has been *glorious* in its variety; it has the more displayed the manifold and unsearchable wisdom of God, and wrought more charity among his people (*Narrative*, 357).

And Mack Stiles: "Temptations to Pragmatism. CPM can fuel in many missionaries desires for results and numbers and dramatic stories." ("What Could Be Wrong with 'Church Planting'? Six Dangers in a Missions Strategy" https://www.desiringgod.org/articles/what-could-be-wrong-with-church-planting. August 24, 2020.)

A second criterion of Edwards worth discussing is **impressions** on the imagination. Many testimonies and accounts of movements include instances of subjective spiritual impressions taken as the Lord's leading, which have led to positive kingdom outcomes.[8] Critiques of movements have not generally cited such impressions as a concern or negative factor in their assessment of movements, but some might hold such concerns, and this factor figured prominently in Edwards own assessment of concerns related to the Awakening, so I mention its relevance here. Edwards had concerns about the role of such impressions (as will be discussed in greater depth later), but he clarified that he considered the presence of such impressions as no argument against a phenomenon being a work of God.

> It is no argument that an operation on the minds of a people, is not the work of the Spirit of God, that many who are the subjects of it, have great impressions made on their imag-

---

[8] For example, the Walker family, describing one movement in Asia, lists as the first of seven key factors in progress: "Listening prayer. Praying is our job. The Lord has changed and adjusted our approaches many times through prayer. Listening is an important part of prayer. There have been so many changes along the way. So many questions: What's next? Shall we work with this person? We've hit a 'roadblock'; what Scriptures shall we use for the next training? Is this a good use of our funding? Is it time to release this brother who's not applying the model, or shall we give him one more chance? Should we continue training in this city or is this a dead end? We, the entire team, have learned to sit and wait for God's answer, no matter what the question." ("How God is Sweeping through South Asia," in *24:14 – A Testimony to All Peoples*, 127-128.)

inations. That persons have many impressions on their imaginations, does not prove that they have nothing else. It is easy to be accounted for, that there should be much of this nature amongst a people, where a great multitude of all kinds of constitutions have their minds engaged with intense thought and strong affections about invisible things; yea, it would be strange if there should not (*Marks*, 262-263).

A third sign worth mention which, according to Edwards, should not discredit a phenomenon, he labels **"imprudences"**: things we would now describe as lacking discretion, wisdom, or good judgment. In some cases, proponents of movements have been accused of making statements lacking in discretion, wisdom, or biblical soundness.[9] Such accusations rarely consist of quo-

---

[9] For example, Aubry Smith: "I argue that the Watsons' non-incarnational, disembodied theology results in devaluing the biblical role of teacher, leads to egregious hermeneutical issues, and violates principles related to contextualization by unconsciously importing foreign cultural values. These issues may affect long-term health of churches emerging from DBS groups." ("Disembodied Discipleship: A Critique of the Discovery Bible Study Method." *EMQ*, April–June 2021, 57:2.)

Also, Darren Carlson: "If we take away all the stories Trousdale tells we can boil down a significant critique to one question – how should we read the Bible? This, of course, is a complex question but from my theological vantage point, Trousdale's entire system could be misleading. A "Gospels-centered" approach to reading the Bible takes its cue from classic liberalism and can turn Jesus into merely a moral teacher. The cross becomes part of the message to obey instead of the message that redeems

tations from leaders within the movements themselves. Most often, problematic quotations come from trainers or Western proponents of movements. And thankfully, the imprudences of which movement proponents are accused consist of unhelpful *statements* rather than unhelpful conduct. Yet we might see some relevance in Edwards' comments about imprudences.

> It is no sign that a work is not from the Spirit of God, that many, who seem to be the subjects of it, are guilty of great imprudences and irregularities in their conduct. We are to consider that the end for which God pours out his Spirit, is to make men holy, and not to make them politicians. Is it no wonder that, in a mixed multitude of all sorts—wise and unwise, young and old, of weak and strong natural abilities, under strong impressions of mind—there are many who behave themselves imprudently. There are but few that know how to conduct them under vehement affections of any kind, whether of a temporal or spiritual nature; to do so requires a great deal of discretion, strength, and steadiness of mind. A

---

dead sinners. It's not that Trousdale is liberal, but that he mimics the methodology." In "A Review of a Popular Missions Book: Miraculous Movements," *Journal of Global Christianity,* August 2015.

And George Terry: "Trousdale's scheme,... similar to T4T in its excessive pragmatism, invalid hermeneutic, and shallow contextualization..." In "A Missiology of Excluded Middles: An Analysis of the T4T Scheme for Evangelism and Discipleship," *Themelios*, 42:2, 341.

> thousand imprudences will not prove a work to be not of the Spirit of God; yea, if there be not only imprudences, but many things prevailing that are irregular, and really contrary to the rules of God's holy word. That it should be thus may be well accounted for from the exceeding weakness of human nature, together with the remaining darkness and corruption of those that are yet the subjects of the saving influences of God's Spirit, and have a real zeal for God.
>
> We have a remarkable instance, in the New Testament, of a people that partook largely of that great effusion of the Spirit in the apostles' days, among whom there nevertheless abounded imprudences and great irregularities; viz. the church at Corinth. (*Marks*, 264)

Since many of the "imprudences" cited consist of statements accused of being biblically erroneous, we move next to Edwards' fourth criterion: "**errors**." Those who best know the details of movements have sometimes said, "Movements are messy."[10] Rapidly-growing movements have many new believers, and new believers are, by definition, not yet mature in their faith and spiritual understanding. Critics of movements have frequently expressed a concern that rapid growth unaccompanied by extensive theological teaching might result in a vari-

---

[10] For example, Trevor Larsen et. al: "What God is doing is exciting, diverse and often messy, but there are a number of key Fruitful Practices that occur again and again in these movements." (*Focus On Fruit - Case Studies and Fruitful Practices*, www.focusonfruit.org, 15.)

ety of errors (syncretism, heresy, or false teaching).[11] Specific examples of such have rarely been cited, yet this concern seems to resonate with many theologically trained commentators. Edwards pointed out that the presence of some errors, even "many delusions of Satan" should not nullify a positive assessment of a phenomenon as a work of God. Thus, Edwards writes,

> Nor are many errors in judgment, and some delusions of Satan intermixed with the work, any argument that the work in general is not of the Spirit of God. However great a spiritual influence may be, it is not to be expected that the Spirit of God should be given now in the same manner as to the apostles, infallibly to

---

[11] For example, Matt Rhodes: "The missionary might report exponentially explosive statistics back home. Yet what he's actually produced may be a burned-over district for the gospel, or, worse, a circus of heresies where a generation of people are now inoculated against the real gospel because they were fooled by a substitute." (*No Shortcut to Success: A Manifesto for Modern Missions* (9Marks). Wheaton, IL: Crossway, 2021, 106.)
Also, Mack Stiles, op.cit.: "Vulnerability to Error and Heresy. The second deep concern I have is that, since mature teachers and preachers are sidelined in the CPM model in the name of indigeneity, the fellowships can be susceptible to wolves and charlatans. Consistently over time, I have seen indigenous churches and individual believers destroyed by outside cults and inside heresy."
And Aubrey Sequeira: "The craze for numbers and the push for rapid growth results in "churches" that have no gospel, no trained leadership, no theology, and no depth—making them easy prey for the heresies of prosperity theology, syncretism, and other false teachings." In "A Plea for Gospel Sanity in Missions."

guide them in points of Christian doctrine, so that what they taught might be relied on as a rule to the Christian church. And if many delusions of Satan appear, at the same time that a great religious concern prevails, it is not an argument that the work in general is not the work of God, any more than it was an argument in Egypt, that there were no true miracles wrought there, by the hand of God, because Jannes and Jambres wrought false miracles at the same time by the hand of the devil. Yea, the same persons may be the subjects of much of the influences of the Spirit of God, and yet in some things be led away by the delusions of Satan, and this be no more of paradox than many other things that are true of real saints, in the present state, where grace dwells with so much corruption, and the new man and the old man subsist together in the same person (*Marks*, 265).

A fifth relevant sign Edwards mentions is **false believers**. This concern has frequently been raised in critiquing movements, especially in light of large numbers of disciples being reported.[12] Most notably con-

---

[12] For example, Matt Rhodes: "In the same way, amateur missions work can leave behind immature converts, unformed churches, and untaught disciples. Even worse, it can leave behind unconverted converts, false churches, and disciples who don't know whom they're supposed to be following. We may mistakenly assume that people have believed or rejected the gospel when in fact they've never understood it." Ibid, 41-42.

cerning Muslim contexts, the question has been raised whether those reporting the numbers have fundamentally misunderstood the nature of the affirmation being made by Muslims professing Christ. Since orthodox Islamic teaching holds *Isa al-Masih* (Jesus) in high regard as a great prophet, perhaps Muslims have seen or heard a message about Jesus, agreed to a favorable attitude toward Jesus, and optimistic evangelists have counted as converts people who in fact don't understand salvation by grace through faith, or the deity of Christ.[13] However, many movements make a point of not counting "converts," but rather "disciples" (those following Christ). Also, this accusation generally arises as an anecdotally-based accusation or *fear* or *suspicion* rather than an evidence-based criticism of reality in movements. Additional study and gathering of solid data from movements is welcome and is underway. Yet concern about the danger of false believers in movements has been mentioned frequently enough that Edwards' observation bears consideration.

---

[13] As in this report from Elliot Clark of his conversation with a missionary working among an unreached people group in North Africa. "In his experience, the gospel is easily obscured by such methods. And he's concerned by Muslims he's seen who, when coming to Christ, are simply converting to a different system of works. They may pray differently. They may give differently. They may even elevate the commands of Jesus and pass them on to others. But they're simply continuing in a modification of the same works-based religion. They've mastered obedience. But he wonders if they know Christ. He's not sure they have the Spirit." *Mission Affirmed* (Wheaton, IL: Crossway, 2022), 125-126.

If some, who were thought to be wrought upon, fall away into gross errors, or scandalous practices, it is no argument that the work in general is not the work of the Spirit of God. That there are some counterfeits, is no argument that nothing is true: such things are always expected in a time of reformation. If we look into church history, we shall find no instance of any great revival of religion, but what has been attended with many such things. Instances of this nature in the apostles' days were innumerable; some fell away into gross heresies, others into vile practices, though they seemed to be the subjects of a work of the Spirit—and were accepted for a while amongst those that were truly so, as their brethren and companions—and were not suspected till they went out from them. And some of these were teachers and officers—and eminent persons in th e Christian church—whom God had endowed with miraculous gifts of the Holy Ghost.... So in the time of the reformation from popery, how great was the number of those who for a while seemed to join with the reformers, yet fell away into the grossest and most absurd errors, and abominable practices.... Therefore the devil's sowing such tares is no proof that a true work of the Spirit of God is not gloriously carried on (*Marks*, 265).

2

Distinguishing Scripture Evidences of a Work of the Spirit of God

Having addressed numerous concerns which should *not* be used to judge whether or not something is from the Spirit of God, Edwards then lists **five sure evidences** that a work *is* from the Spirit of God. All five have relevance for any assessment of movements in our day. I will simply quote excerpts of these without comment, and leave it to each reader to weigh what they know of any movement(s) in light of these evidences.

> Having shown, in some instances, what are not evidences that a work wrought among a people, is not a work of the Spirit of God, I now proceed, in the second place, as was proposed, to show positively, what are the sure, distinguishing scripture evidences and marks of a work of the Spirit of God, by which we may proceed in judging of any operation we find in ourselves, or see among a people, without danger of being misled.—And in this, as I said before, I shall confine myself wholly to those marks which are given us by the apostle in the chapter wherein is my text, where this matter

is particularly handled, and more plainly and fully than anywhere else in the Bible. And in speaking to these marks, I shall take them in the order in which I find them in the chapter.

I. When the operation is such as to raise their esteem of that Jesus who was born of the Virgin, and was crucified without the gates of Jerusalem; and seems more to confirm and establish their minds in the truth of what the gospel declares to us of his being the Son of God, and the Saviour of men; is a sure sign that it is from the Spirit of God. This sign the apostle gives us in the 2d and 3d verses,. "Hereby know ye the Spirit of God; and every spirit that confesseth that Jesus Christ is come in the flesh is of God; and every spirit that confesseth not that Jesus Christ is come in the flesh is not of God" (*Marks*, 266).

So that if the spirit that is at work among a people is plainly observed to work so as to convince them of Christ, and lead them to him—to confirm their minds in the belief of the history of Christ as he appeared in the flesh—and that he is the Son of God, and was sent of God to save sinners; that he is the only Saviour, and that they stand in great need of him; and if he seems to beget in them higher and more honourable thoughts of him than they used to have, and to incline their

affections more to him; it is a sure sign that it is the true and right Spirit; however incapable we may be to determine, whether that conviction and affection be in that manner, or to that degree, as to be saving or not (*Marks*, 266).
II. When the spirit that is at work operates against the interests of Satan's kingdom, which lies in encouraging and establishing sin, and cherishing men's worldly lusts; this is a sure sign that it is a true, and not a false spirit (*Marks*, 267).
III. The spirit that operates in such a manner, as to cause in men a greater regard to the Holy Scriptures, and establishes them more in their truth and divinity, is certainly the Spirit of God (*Marks*, 267).
IV. Another rule to judge of spirits may be drawn from those compellations given to the opposite spirits, in the last words of the 6th verse, "The spirit of truth and the spirit of error." These words exhibit the two opposite characters of the Spirit of God, and other spirits that counterfeit his operations. And therefore, if by observing the manner of the operation of a spirit that is at work among a people, we see that it operates as a spirit of truth, leading persons to truth, convincing them of those things that are true, we may safely determine that it is a right and true spirit (*Marks*, 268).

Whatever spirit removes our darkness, and brings us to the light, undeceives us, and, by convincing us of the truth, doth us a kindness. If I am brought to a sight of truth, and am made sensible of things as they really are, my duty is immediately to thank God for it, without standing first to inquire by what means I have such a benefit (*Marks*, 268).

V. If the spirit that is at work among a people operates as a spirit of love to God and man, it is a sure sign that it is the Spirit of God. This sign the apostle insists upon from the 6th verse to the end of the chapter. "Beloved, let us love one another; for love is of God, and every one that loveth is born of God, and knoweth God: he that loveth not, knoweth not God; for God is love," &c. (*Marks*, 268).

Thus, I have spoken particularly to the several marks the apostle gives us of a work of the true Spirit. There are some of these things which the devil *would not* do if he could: thus he would not awaken the conscience, and make men sensible of their miserable state by reason of sin, and sensible of their great need of a Saviour; and he would not confirm men in the belief that Jesus is the Son of God, and the Saviour of sinners, or raise men's value and esteem of him: he would not beget in men's minds an opinion of the necessity, usefulness, and truth of the Holy Scriptures, or incline them to make much use of them; nor would he show men the truth, in things that concern their souls' interest; to undeceive them, and lead them out of darkness into light, and give them a view of things as they really are. And there are other things that the devil *neither can nor will* do; he will not give men a spirit of divine love, or Christian humility and poverty of spirit; nor *could* he if he would. He cannot give those things he has not himself: these things are as contrary as possible to his nature (*Marks*, 269).

These marks, that the apostle has given us, are sufficient to stand alone, and support themselves. They plainly show *the finger of God*, and are sufficient to outweigh a thousand such little objections, as many make from oddities, irregularities, errors in conduct, and the delusions and scandals of some professors.

But here some may *object* to the sufficiency of the marks given, what the apostle Paul says in 2 Cor. xi. 13, 14. "For such are false apostles, deceitful workers, transforming themselves into the apostles of Christ; and no marvel, for Satan himself is transformed into an angel of light."

To which I *answer*, that this can be no objection against the sufficiency of these marks to distinguish the true from the

> false spirit, in those false apostles and prophets, in whom the devil was transformed into an angel of light, because it is principally with a view to them that the apostle gives these marks; as appears by the words of the text, "Believe not every spirit, but try the spirits, whether they are of God;" and this is the reason he gives, because many false prophets are gone out into the world (*Marks*, 269).

As already noted, some critics of movements have strongly objected to the use of any methodology not explicitly commanded or modeled in Scripture.[14] Edwards' "Thoughts on the Revival" strongly exhorts readers not to judge a work by the methods employed, but rather to consider the fruit borne from it. He begins the essay thus:

PART I.

SHOWING THAT THE EXTRAORDINARY WORK THAT HAS OF LATE BEEN GOING ON IN THIS LAND, IS A GLORIOUS WORK OF GOD.

The error of those who have had ill thoughts

---

[14] Vegas and Kocman go so far as to say: "It is our contention that a proper understanding of the biblical gospel necessitates a ministry methodology understood, employed, and taught by the apostle Paul." Ibid, 119. If actually applied, this would of course exclude any use of complete Bibles or modern technology, such as mass printing, satellite, internet, radio, television, telephone, or any other device requiring electricity.

of the great religious operation on the minds of men, that has been carried on of late in *New England* (so far as the ground of such an error has been in the understanding, and not in the disposition,) seems fundamentally to lie in three things: *First* In judging of this work *a priori. Secondly*, In not taking the holy scriptures as a whole rule whereby to judge of such operations. *Thirdly*, In not justly separating and distinguishing the good from the bad.

SECT. I.

We should not judge of this work by the supposed causes, but by the effects.

They have greatly erred in the way in which they have gone about to try this work, whether it be a work of the Spirit of God or no, viz. in judging of it *a priori* ; from the way that it *began*, the *instruments* that have been employed, the *means* that have been made use of, and the methods that have been taken and succeeded in carrying it on. Whereas, if we duly consider the matter, it will evidently appear that such a work is not to be judged of *a priori*, but *a posteriori* : we are to observe the *effect* wrought ; and if, upon examination of it, it be found to be agreeable to the word of God, we are bound, without more ado, to rest in it as God's work ; and shall be like to be rebuked for our arrogance, if we refuse so to do till God shall explain to us how he has brought this effect to pass, or why he has made use of such and such means in doing it.

These texts are enough to cause us with trembling to forbear such a way of proceeding in judging of a work of God's Spirit: Isa. xl. 13, 14. "Who hath directed the Spirit of the Lord, or being his counselor hath taught him? With whom took he counsel, and who instructed him, and who taught him in the path of judgment, and taught him knowledge, and showed to him the way of understanding?" John iii. 8. " The wind bloweth where it listeth, and thou hearest the sound thereof, but canst not tell whence it cometh, and whither it goeth." We hear the sound, we perceive the effect, and from thence we judge that the wind does indeed blow; without waiting before we pass this judgment, first, to be satisfied what should be the cause of the wind's blowing from such a part of the heavens, and how it should come to pass that it should blow in such a manner, at such a time. To judge *a priori*, is a wrong way of judging of any of the works of God." (*Thoughts*, 366)

3
Practical Inferences

Having addressed negative signs and elucidated "the sure, distinguishing scripture evidences and marks of a work of the Spirit of God," Edwards presents three practical inferences of those truths.

> I. From what has been said, I will venture to draw this inference, *viz. That the extraordinary influence that has lately appeared, causing an uncommon concern and engagedness of mind about the things of religion, is undoubtedly, in the general, from the Spirit of God* (Marks, 269).
>
> And here I would observe, that the nature and tendency of a spirit that is at work, may be determined with much greater certainty, and less danger of being imposed upon, when it is observed in a great multitude of people of all sorts, and in various places, than when it is only seen in a few, in some particular place, that have been much conversant one with another. A few particular persons may agree to put a cheat upon others, by

a false pretense, and professing things of which they never were conscious. But when the work is spread over great parts of a country, in places distant from one another, among people of all sorts and of all ages, and in multitudes possessed of a sound mind, good understanding, and known integrity; there would be the greatest absurdity in supposing, from all the observation that can be made by all that is heard from and seen in them—for many months together, and by those who are most intimate with them in these affairs, and have long been acquainted with them—that yet it cannot be determined what kind of influence the operation they are under, has upon people's minds, can it not be determined whether it tends to awaken their consciences, or to stupify them; whether it inclines them more to seek their salvation, or neglect it; whether it seems to confirm them in a belief of the Scriptures, or to lead them to deism; whether it makes them have more regard for the great truths of religion, or less? (*Marks*, 270).

But whether persons' convictions, and the alteration in their dispositions and affections, be in a degree and manner that is saving, is beside the present question. If there be such effects on people's judgments, dispositions, and affections, as

> have been spoken of, whether they be in a degree and manner that is saving or no, it is nevertheless a sign of the influence of the Spirit of God. Scripture rules serve to distinguish the common influences of the Spirit of God, as well as those that are saving, from the influence of other causes (*Marks*, 270).

Edwards argues, based on the *general* change in many people's character and affections, that "whether they be in a degree and manner that is saving or no, it is nevertheless a sign of the influence of the Spirit of God." He then mentions the biblical guidelines (rules) that enable discernment of saving influences. Thus, while offering pastoral words of counsel and caution along the way, he presents his conclusion that the phenomena taking place in his time and ministry context were "*in the general, from the Spirit of God.*" In this he reflects the spirit of Barnabas the encourager who, "When he arrived and saw what the grace of God had done [in Antioch], he was glad and encouraged them all to remain true to the Lord with all their hearts" (Acts 11:23).

Some have considered it overzealous advocacy to describe movements as "a work of God."[15] Edwards felt no such compunction about using such a description for the awakening taking place in his time, as will be seen numerous times in the following quotations. Having applied Edwards' negative signs and sure evidences to current phenomena as much as relevant, it seems

---
[15] Private correspondence with various movement critics.

appropriate for us to follow his cue and acknowledge that the phenomena being described as Church Planting Movements and Disciple Making Movements are *in general from the Spirit of God.*

Following from his first inference, Edwards offers strong words of warning.

> II. Let us all be hence warned, *by no means to oppose, or do any thing in the least to clog or hinder, the work; but, on the contrary, do our utmost to promote it.* Now Christ is come down from heaven in a remarkable and wonderful work of his Spirit, it becomes all his professed disciples to acknowledge him, and give him honour.
>
> The example of the Jews in Christ's and the apostles' times, is enough to beget in those who do not acknowledge this work, a great jealousy of themselves, and to make them exceeding cautious of what they say or do (*Marks*, 272).
>
> They were *astonished* by what they saw and heard, but not *convinced.* And especially was the work of God then rejected by those that were most conceited of their own understanding and knowledge, agreeable to Isa. xxix. 14. "Therefore, behold, I will proceed to do a marvellous work amongst this people, even a marvellous work and a wonder; for the wisdom of their wise men shall perish, and the understanding of their

prudent men shall be hid." And many who had been in reputation for religion and piety, had a great spite against the work, because they saw it tended to diminish their honour, and to reproach their formality and lukewarmness (*Marks*, 272).

I would entreat those who quiet themselves, that they proceed on a principle of prudence, and are waiting to see the issue of things—and what fruits those that are the subjects of this work will bring forth in their lives and conversations—to consider, whether this will justify a long refraining form acknowledging Christ when he appears so wonderfully and graciously present in the land.... If they wait to see a work of God without difficulties and stumbling-blocks, it will be like the fool's waiting at the river side to have the water all run by. A work of God without stumbling-blocks is never to be expected. "It must need be that offences come." There never yet was any great manifestation that God made of himself to the world, without many difficulties attending it (*Marks*, 273).

Those who are now waiting to see the issue of this work, think they shall be better able to determine by and by; but probably many of them are mistaken. The Jews that saw Christ's miracles, waited to see better evidences of his being the

Messiah; they wanted a sign from heaven; but they waited in vain; their stumbling-blocks did not diminish, but increase. They found no end to them, and so were more and more hardened in unbelief. Many have been praying for that glorious reformation spoken of in Scripture, who knew not what they have been praying for, (as it was with the Jews when they prayed for the coming of Christ,) and who, if it should come, would not acknowledge or receive it.

This pretended prudence, in persons waiting so long before they acknowledged this work, will probably in the end prove the greatest imprudence. Hereby they will fail of any share of so great a blessing, and will miss the most precious opportunity of obtaining divine light, grace, and comfort, heavenly and eternal benefits, that God ever gave in New England. While the glorious fountain is set open in so wonderful a manner, and multitudes flock to it and receive a rich supply for the wants of their souls, they stand at a distance, doubting, wondering, and receiving nothing, and are like to continue thus till the precious season is past (*Marks*, 273).

Whether what has been said in this discourse be enough to produce conviction, that this is the work of God or not; yet I

> hope that for the future, they will at least hearken to the caution of Gamaliel, now mentioned; so as not to oppose it, or say any thing which has even an indirect tendency to bring it into discredit, lest they should be found opposers of the Holy Ghost (*Marks*, 273).
>
> Since the great God has come down from heaven, and manifested himself in so wonderful a manner in this land, it is vain for any of us to expect any other than to be greatly affected by it in our spiritual state and circumstances, respecting the favour of God, one way or other. Those who do not become more happy by it, will become far more guilty and miserable (*Marks*, 273).

In "Thoughts on the Revival," Edwards sounds similar notes of warning, at some length:

> There are many things in the word of God, showing that when God remarkably appears in any great work for his church, and against his enemies, it is a most dangerous thing, and highly provoking to God, to be slow and backward to acknowledge and honor God in the work (*Thoughts*, 380).
>
> The church of Christ is called upon greatly to rejoice, when at any time Christ remarkably appears, coming to his church, to carry on the work of salvation, to enlarge his own

kingdom, and to deliver poor souls out of the pit wherein there is no water (*Thoughts*, 381).

The great danger of not appearing openly to acknowledge, rejoice in, and promote that great work of God, in bringing in that glorious harvest, is represented in Zech. xiv. 16, 17, 18, 19 (*Thoughts*, 383).

As persons will greatly expose themselves to the curse of God, by opposing, or standing at a distance, and keeping silence at such a time as this; so for persons to arise, and readily to acknowledge God, and honor him in such a work, and cheerfully and vigorously to exert themselves to promote it, will be to put themselves much in the way of the divine blessing (*Thoughts*, 386).

Though ministers preach never so good doctrine, and are never so painful and laborious in their work, yet, if at such a day as this, they show to their people, that they are not well-affected to this work, but are very doubtful and suspicious of it, they will be very likely to do their people a great deal more hurt than good (*Thoughts*, 388).

It is our wisest and best way, fully, and without reluctance, to bow to the great God in this work, and to be entirely resigned to him, with respect to the manner in which he carries it on, and the instruments he is pleased to use. Let us not to show ourselves out of humor, and sullenly to refuse to acknowledge the work, in its full glory, because we have not had so great a hand in promoting it, or have not shared so largely in its blessings, as some others; and not to refuse to give all that honor that belongs to others as instruments, because they are young, or are upon other accounts much inferior to ourselves and others; and may appear to us very unworthy, that God should put so much honor upon them (*Thoughts*, 389).

Instead of coming to the help of the Lord, we shall actually fight against him, if we are abundant in insisting on and setting forth the blemishes of the work, so as to manifest that we rather choose, and are more forward to take notice of what is amiss, than what is good and glorious in the work. Not but that the errors that are committed, ought to be observed and lamented, and a proper testimony borne against them, and the most probable means should be used to have them amended; but an insisting much upon them, as though it were a pleasing theme, or speaking of them with more appearance of heat of spirit, or with ridicule, or an air of contempt, than grief for them, has no tendency to correct the errors; but has a tendency to darken the glory of God's power and grace, appearing in the substance of the work, and to beget jealousies and ill thoughts in the minds of others concerning the whole of it (*Thoughts*, 389-390).

Whatever errors many zealous persons have run into, yet if the work, in the substance of it, be the work of God, then it is a joyful day indeed; it is so in heaven, and ought to be so among God's people on earth, especially in that part of the earth where this glorious work is carried on. It is a day of great rejoicing with Christ himself: the good Shepherd, when he finds his sheep that was lost, lays it on his shoulders rejoicing, and calls together his friends and neighbors, saying, *Rejoice with me*. If we therefore are Christ's friends, now it should be a day of great rejoicing with us. If we viewed things in a just light, so great an event as the conversion of such a multitude of sinners, would draw and engage our attention much more than all the imprudencies and irregularities that have been; our hearts would be swallowed up with the glory of this event, and we should have no great disposition to attend to any thing else. The imprudencies and errors of poor feeble worms do not hinder or prevent great rejoicing, in the presence of the angels of God, over so many poor sinners that have repented; and it will be an argument of something very ill in us, if they prevent our rejoicing.

Who loves, in a day of great joy and gladness, to be much insisting on those things that are uncomfortable?.... Would it be agreeable to the bridegroom, on the day of his espousals, the day of the gladness of his heart, to be much insisting on the blemishes of his bride? (*Thoughts*, 390).

> This work, which has lately been carried on in the land, is the work of God, and not the work of man. Its beginning has not been of man's power or device, and its being carried on depends not on our strength or wisdom; but yet God expects of all, that they should use their utmost endeavors to promote it, and that the hearts of all should be greatly engaged in this affair. We should improve our utmost strength in it, however vain human strength is without the power of God; and so he no less requires that we should improve our utmost care, wisdom, and prudence, though human wisdom, of itself, be as vain as human strength. Though God is wont to carry on such a work, in such a manner as many ways to show the weakness and vanity of means and human endeavors in themselves; yet, at the same time, he carries it on in such a manner as to encourage diligence and vigilance in the use of proper means and endeavors, and to punish the neglect of them. Therefore, in our endeavors to promote this great work, we ought to use the utmost caution, vigilance, and skill, in the measures we take in order to it (*Thoughts*, 390).

If, in fact, God is at work in movements, Edwards' words of warning may apply to those inclined to oppose movements, more than affirming or encouraging them. Words of friendly caution, such as Edwards turns to next, differ in character from opposition, verbal attack, or even the "wait and see" attitude against which he warns.

In his third inference, Edwards offers cautionary advice to friends of the work: both those who have been directly involved in it, and those zealous to promote it. A good deal of this advice, though not all, seems relevant to modern Church Planting Movements. He offers first a general and fitting word of caution, to avoid errors and misconduct.

> III. To apply myself to those who are the friends of this work, who have been partakers of it, and are zealous to promote it. Let me earnestly exhort such to give diligent heed to themselves to avoid all errors and misconduct, and whatever may darken and obscure the work; and to give no occasion to those who stand ready to reproach it (*Marks*, 273).

Whenever we have any connection with a great work of God, we need humility and caution lest pride lead us to claim any credit for the work the Lord is graciously doing. Edwards offers this prescription:

> Humility and self-diffidence, and an entire dependence on our Lord Jesus Christ, will be our best defense. Let us therefore maintain the strictest watch against spiritual pride, or being lifted up with extraordinary experiences and comforts, and the high favours of heaven, that any of us may have received (*Marks*, 274).

JONATHAN EDWARDS ON MOVEMENTS

In "Thoughts on the Revival," Edwards offers similar counsel concerning the vital need for humility and great care to avoid spiritual pride. This can usefully be applied by all of us, regardless of our stance on movements, and however that stance might pull us toward some form of spiritual pride.

> Since therefore the errors of the friends and promoters of such a glorious work of God are of such dreadful consequence; and seeing the devil, being sensible of this, is so assiduous, watchful, and subtle in his attempts with them, and has thereby been so successful to overthrow religion heretofore; certainly such persons ought to be exceeding circumspect and vigilant, diffident and jealous of themselves, and humbly dependent on the guidance of the good Shepherd (*Thoughts*, 398).
>
> The errors that attend a great revival of religion, usually arise from these three things. 1. Undiscerned spiritual pride; 2. Wrong principles; and 3. Ignorance of Satan's advantages and devices.... The first, and the worst cause of errors, that prevail in such a state of things, is *spiritual pride*. This is the main door by which the devil comes into the hearts of those that are zealous for the advancement of religion" (*Thoughts*, 398-399).

Edwards boldly encourages others to *promote* the work taking place in the awakening. I believe we would do well to heed his advice for promotion of God's work in our day.

> I now proceed to show positively, what ought to be done...to promote this work. .... That which I think we ought to set ourselves about in the first place, is to remove stumbling-blocks.... And in order to this, there must be a great deal done at confessing of faults, on both sides: for undoubtedly many and great are the faults that have been committed, in the jangling and confusions, and mixtures of light and darkness, that have been of late (*Thoughts*, 421).

Perhaps such a suggestion could serve as an encouragement toward brotherly dialogue between those inclined to feel excited about movements and those inclined to feel concerned.

Edwards next picks up a theme he had mentioned among the negative signs that do not negate a work being of God: **subjective impressions** taken as guidance from the Lord.

> Some of the true friends of the work of God's Spirit have erred in giving too much heed to impulses and strong impressions on their minds, as though they were immediate significations from heaven to them, of something that should come to pass, or something that it was the mind and will of God that they should do, which was not signified or

revealed any where in the Bible without those impulses. These impressions, if they are truly from the Spirit of God, are of a quite different nature from his gracious influences on the hearts of the saints: they are of the nature of the extraordinary *gifts* of the Spirit, and are properly inspiration, such as the prophets and apostles and others had of old; which the apostle distinguishes from the *grace* of the Spirit, 1 Cor. xiii. (*Marks*, 274).

As previously mentioned, many testimonies and accounts of movements include instances of subjective spiritual impressions taken as the Lord's leading, which have led to positive kingdom outcomes. Such occurrences are not unique to movements. Receiving guidance from subjective spiritual impressions takes place among many Christians all around the world, and has been practiced in some form by many Christians throughout Church history. Certainly, in some cases (historically and globally), these impressions have led to folly, and have been inadequately tested by the infallible guidance of Scripture. But Edwards' strong warning against finding *any value* in such impressions finds its roots in his cessationist theology. He expresses his conviction that all miraculous "extraordinary" gifts had ceased and become unnecessary, since the church had reached a stage of maturity greater than what it possessed in its early years. He also identifies subjective spiritual impressions as a type of inspired prophecy, carrying with them great danger.

One erroneous principle, than which scarce any has proved more mischievous to the present glorious work of God, is a notion that it is God's manner, now in these days, to guide his saints, at least some that are more eminent, by inspiration, or immediate revelation, and to make known to them what shall come to pass hereafter, or what it is his will that they should do, by impressions made upon their minds, either with or without texts of Scripture; whereby something is made known to them, that is not taught in the Scripture (*Thoughts*, 404).

The ordinary sanctifying influences of the Spirit of God are the *end* of all extraordinary gifts, as the apostle shows, Ephes. iv. 11, 12, 13. They are good for nothing, any further than as they are subordinate to this end; they will be so far from profiting any without it, that they will only aggravate their misery. This is, as the apostle observes, the most excellent way of God's communicating his Spirit to his church, it is the greatest glory of the church in all ages. This glory is what makes the church on earth most like the church in heaven, when prophecy, and tongues, and other miraculous gifts, cease. And God communicates his Spirit only in that more excellent way of which the apostle speaks, viz. charity or divine love, "which never faileth." Therefore the glory of the approaching happy state of the church does not at all require these extraordinary gifts. As that state of the church will be nearest of any to its perfect state in heaven, so I believe it will be like it in this, that all extraordinary gifts shall have ceased and vanished away; and all those stars, and the moon with the reflected light they gave in the night, or in a dark season, shall be swallowed up in the sun of divine love. The apostle speaks of these gifts of inspiration as childish things, in comparison of the influence of the Spirit in divine love; things given to the church only to support it in its minority, till the church should have a complete standing rule established, and all the ordinary means of grace should be settled; but as things that should cease, as the church advanced to the state of manhood. 1 Cor. xiii. 11. "When I was a child, I spake as a child, I understood as a child, I thought as a child; but when I became a man, I put away childish things;" compared with the three preceding verses.

When the apostle, in this chapter, speaks of prophecies, tongues, and revelations ceasing, and vanishing away in the church—when the Christian church should be advanced from a state of minority to a state of manhood—he seems to have respect to its coming to an adult state in this world, as well as in heaven; for he speaks of such a state of manhood, wherein those three things, Faith, Hope, and Charity, should remain after miracles and revelation had ceased (*Marks*, 274-275).

> Therefore I do not expect a restoration of these miraculous gifts in the approaching glorious times of the church, nor do I desire it. It appears to me, that it would add nothing to the glory of those times, but rather diminish from it (*Marks*, 275).

Sam Storms comments:

> Jonathan Edwards was a cessationist. Largely because of excessive and fanatical behavior associated with the way in which certain people justified unwise, even unbiblical, decisions by appealing to having heard "the voice of God." He also opposed the contemporary validity of revelatory gifts (especially prophecy) because he believed, falsely in my opinion, that such would undermine the finality and sufficiency of Scripture. I mention this only to point out that, although I disagree with Edwards on this issue, his belief didn't diminish in the least his love and appreciation for the Holy Spirit (*Storms*, 202).

Other conservative and Reformed scholars, such as Wayne Grudem,[16] have argued (convincingly in my opin-

---

[16] See Grudem, Wayne. 2000. *The Gift of Prophecy in the New Testament and Today*. Wheaton, IL: Crossway;
Grudem, Wayne. 2000. *The Gift of Prophecy in 1 Corinthians*. Eugene, OR: Wipf and Stock;
Grudem, Wayne. 1994. "Gifts of the Holy Spirit," in *Systematic Theology*. Grand Rapids, MI: Zondervan. 1016-1083.

ion) for the validity of subjective spiritual impressions which, while fallible and in need of testing and discernment, can be useful means of God's work in his people's lives. As previously mentioned, debate about the validity and usefulness of such impressions ranges far wider (both globally and historically) than discussion about movements. However, since these phenomena often play a significant role in movements and Edwards cautions quite strongly concerning them, the issue seems worth bringing into the light and examining with appropriate clarity.

On a related note, Edwards cautions against scorning natural **application of human wisdom** – in all things, including in our approaches to ministry. We should plan well and wisely, do good research, and apply whatever insights can be gained from human learning.

> Moreover, seeing inspiration is not to be expected, *let us not despise human learning.* They who assert that human learning is of little or no use in the work of the ministry, do not well consider what they say; if they did, they would not say it. By human learning I mean, and suppose others mean, the improvement of common knowledge by human and outward means. (*Marks*, 275).
>
> An increase of knowledge, without doubt, increases a man's advantage either to do good or hurt, according as he is disposed. It is too manifest to be denied, that God made great use of human learning in the apostle Paul, as he also did in Moses and Solomon.

> And if knowledge, obtained by human means, is not to be despised, then it will follow that the means of obtaining it are not to be neglected, viz. *study* (*Marks*, 275).

Edwards also cautions (begs!) against **questioning the salvation of others** who give a credible profession of faith. In his context, he aimed this caution toward those touched by the revival who questioned the salvation of those continuing in a quiet and "lifeless" faith, as they had prior to the revival. I know of no cases of those in movements questioning the salvation of those (who profess salvation by grace through faith in Christ) already attending existing churches. Rather it is opponents of movements who have sometimes publicly questioned the salvation of those coming to biblical faith out of other religious backgrounds.[17] Edwards exhorts:

---

[17] See Rhodes, footnote 12. Also Aubrey Sequeira's critique mixing Insider Movements, church growth and Church Planting Movements: "The push for numbers and rapid growth in missions has resulted in much distortion and dilution of the gospel message today. People are taught to 'believe in Jesus,' 'receive Jesus,' or 'make a decision for Jesus' without any of the biblical teaching on repentance. The so-called 'conversions' that result are nominal at best, manipulative at worst....In many cases, people 'convert' in droves, believing that converting to Christianity will bring them certain social or economic benefits. Missionaries triumphantly send reports back home with testimonies featuring stupendous and unfathomable statistics of people converted and churches established." ("A Plea for Gospel Sanity in Missions," https://www.9marks.org/article/a-plea-for-gospel-sanity-in-missions.)
Also, Vegas and Kocman: "When the attendees of such churches are revealed as false converts years later, few make the logi-

> Another thing I would beg the dear children of God more fully to consider of, is, how far, and upon what grounds, the rules of the Holy Scriptures will truly justify their passing censures upon other professing Christians, as hypocrites, and ignorant of real religion (*Marks*, 275).

He offers similar warnings in "Thoughts on the Revival":

> Censuring others is the worst disease with which this affair has been attended. But this is indeed a time of great temptation to this sinful error (*Thoughts*, 373).
>
> And here the first thing I would take notice of is, censuring professing Christians of good standing in the visible church, as unconverted. I need not repeat what I have elsewhere said to show this to be against the plain, frequent, and strict prohibitions of the word of God: it is the worst disease that has attended this work, most contrary to the spirit and rules of Christianity, and of worst consequences (*Thoughts*, 415).
>
> God seems so strictly to have forbidden our

---

cal connection necessary to call into question the initial methods used to build such ministries." (*Missions by the Book*, 14.) Although the authors level this accusation against Church Planting Movements among unreached people groups, the example they cite refers to "pragmatism in the North American church growth movement."

> judging our brethren in the visible church, not only because he knew that we were infinitely too weak, fallible and blind, to be well capacitated for it, but also because he knew that it was not a work suited to our proud hearts; that it would be setting us vastly too high, and making us too much of lords over our fellow-creatures (*Thoughts*, 416).

Edwards also counsels against **patching the new onto the old**.

> I would humbly recommend to those that love the Lord Jesus Christ, and would advance his kingdom, a good attendance to that excellent rule of prudence which Christ has left us, Matt. ix. 16, 17. "No man putteth a piece of new cloth into an old garment; for that which is put in to fill it up, taketh from the garment, and the rent is made worse. Neither do men put new wine into old bottles; else the bottles break and the wine runneth out, and the bottles perish. But they put new wine into new bottles, and both are preserved." (*Marks*, 276).

This counsel has relevance for the relationship between new house churches developing within movements, and established churches and denominations already existing in various places. While all disciples and churches globally function as part of the body of Christ, it is generally unwise to try to patch new churches into older denominations. One factor contributing to rapid multiplication of new churches and strong discipleship within movements is their indigenous character. They tend to have a local "flavor," effectively applying biblical truths and values within their local context. As they grow, they develop the structures needed for discipleship and effective functioning within their setting. Drawing them into previously established denominations clothes them with ecclesiastical Saul's armor, radically diminishing these young churches' ability to manifest God's kingdom through locally powerful expressions of Christ's body.

On a related note, Edwards counsels God's people to **neither err in being hemmed in by traditional forms nor carried away in fruitless innovation**. To use modern parlance, he encourages all to "keep the main thing the main thing." He advises readers to follow the example of the Apostle Paul, prioritizing contextually flexible gospel proclamation, so that we might *by all means* save some.

> For though I believe we have confined ourselves too much to a certain stated method and form in the management of our religious affairs; which has had a tendency to cause all our religion to degenerate into mere formality; yet whatever has the appearance of a great innovation—that tends much to shock and surprise people's minds, and to set them a talking and disputing—tends greatly to hinder the progress of the power of religion. It raises the opposition of some, diverts the mind of others, and perplexes many with doubts and scruples. It causes people to swerve from their

> great business, and turn aside to vain jangling. Therefore that which is very much beside the common practice, unless it be a thing in its own nature of considerable importance, had better be avoided. Herein we shall follow the example of one who had the greatest success in propagating the power of religion. 1 Cor. ix. 20-23.... "I am made all things to all men, that I might by all means save some. And this I do for the gospel's sake, that I might be partaker thereof with you." (*Marks*, 276-277).

This serves as a fitting conclusion to gleanings from "The Distinguishing Marks of a Work of the Spirit of God." When we recognize the Spirit accomplishing a uniquely fruitful work, we do well to guard against resisting the Spirit's work through criticism based on our previous or traditional forms and patterns of ministry. We also do well to focus on those things that show clear evidence of increasing the glory of Christ – both through bringing his gospel to the lost and through deepening the spiritual maturity of believers. Whatever novelties or innovations do not tend toward these goals may in fact distract and deter from the highest blessings the Lord desires to unleash among his people. Thus as we exercise creativity in ministry, we do well to maintain a focus on the things which are "in [their] own nature of considerable importance."

Having interacted with relevant insights from "Distinguishing Marks," we now turn to some of Edwards' additional comments found in "Thoughts on the Revival," which can offer useful insights into our consideration of modern movements.

4
Additional Insights from "Thoughts on the Revival"

One concern frequently expressed about movements is the element of **rapid multiplication.** Many have cautioned of dangers related to rapid advance in kingdom work.[18] Edwards faced many similar concerns in his

---

[18] See, for example, Aubrey Sequeira: "The craze for numbers and the push for rapid growth results in "churches" that have no gospel, no trained leadership, no theology, and no depth—making them easy prey for the heresies of prosperity theology, syncretism, and other false teachings.... The push for numbers and rapid growth in missions has resulted in much distortion and dilution of the gospel message today." ("A Plea for Gospel Sanity in Missions," https://www.9marks.org/article/a-plea-for-gospel-sanity-in-missions/.)

Also, Brooks Buser and Chad Vegas: "Many are now operating with a goal of finishing the task with rapid speed, based on a misunderstanding of Matthew 24:14....This poorly conceived mission is undermining the long-term work of disciple-making and establishing strong New Testament churches." ("Why Unreached People Groups Still Matter in Missions" www.thegospelcoalition.org/article/why-unreached-people-groups-still-matter-in-missions/.)

And Zane Pratt: "But what it essentially boils down to is a sort of a multi-level marketing idea where you have rapid disciples making disciples, making disciples in a fairly narrow and formulaic fashion that in many ways reduces in my mind discipleship

context. He responded that if a work is from God, its rapid growth and expansion should not cause observers to stumble, but rather to rejoice.

> And that we may be warned not to continue doubting and unbelieving concerning this work, because of the extraordinary degree of it, and the suddenness and swiftness of the accomplishment of the great things that pertain to it; let us consider the example of the unbelieving lord in *Samaria*, who could not believe so extraordinary a work of God to be accomplished so suddenly as was declared to him (*Thoughts*, 385). [2 Kings 7:1-2]
>
> Besides, those things in this work, which have been chiefly complained of as new, are not so new as has been generally imagined. Though they have been much more frequent lately, in proportion to the uncommon degree, extent and swiftness, and other extraordinary circumstances, of the work, yet they are not *new* in their kind, but are things of the same nature as have been found, and well approved of, in the church of God before, from time to time" (*Thoughts*, 369-370).

---

to far less than what it actually is in Scripture." ("Zane Pratt: Are Explosive Disciple-making Movements Really Healthy?" Podcast posted by Alex Kocman, 2 Jul 2018. missionspodcast.com/podcast/zane-pratt-are-explosive-disciple-making-movements-really-healthy.)

Edwards also expressed a concern for maintaining a clear distinction between the **ministry functions of ordinary believers and the ministry functions of ordained clergy**. Active ministry by all disciples ("ordinary people") has been a hallmark of movements and their rapid multiplication.[19] Concerns about this dynamic have been expressed in various forms.[20] I have

---

[19] For example, Samuel Kebreab describes among the features of Disciple Making Movements: "DMMs Involve Ordinary Disciples Making Disciples and Churches Planting Churches." ("Observations Over Fifteen Years of Disciple Making Movements," in *Motus Dei: The Movement of God to Disciple the Nations,* (Pasadena, CA: William Carey Publishing, 2021) 29.)

Victor John testifies: "We also have an 18-year old girl leading a church. Her grandfather is one of the members of the church. God does extraordinary things with ordinary people." (*Bhojpuri Breakthrough: A Movement that Keeps Multiplying.* (Monument, CO: WIGTake Resources, 2019), 172.)

[20] The two most common forms are: 1. questions such as "Who is authorized in these movements to administer baptism and the Lord's Supper?"; and 2. descriptions of the marks of a church, presented in a theological framework in which those marks can only be performed by an ordained person – for example, by Vegas and Kocman: "Protestants have historically argued that the Holy Spirit generally works through ordinary means. Those ordinary means are defined as preaching the Word and administering the ordinances of baptism and the Lord's Supper. The Westminster Confession of Faith summarized this…" (*Missions by the Book,* 59.)

Note also Mark Dever's comment: "I think it was horrible of you to baptize them spontaneously when they're going to burn forever in hell. And I think you should have been much more careful, like Jesus taught. Like we see in the New Testament; like you see pastors being in the New Testament." ("Radius and 9Marks (Mark Dever) on CPM," posted at on October 16, 2019 at https://www.youtube.com/watch?v=fi9Xp8D7_Oc.)

John Massey, on the other hand, bases his objection on cul-

not seen those concerns expressed *explicitly* as a need to maintain a strong clergy-laity distinction (as Edwards frames it), yet that seems to clearly be the assumed framework out of which some objections arise. Thus, I see Edwards' concerns along this line as quite relevant.

> The common people, in exhorting one another, ought not to clothe themselves with the like authority with that which is proper for ministers. There is a certain authority that ministers have, and should exercise in teaching, as well as governing the flock.... Ministers in this work of teaching and exhorting are clothed with authority, as Christ's messengers.... Ministers therefore, in the exercise of this power, may clothe themselves with authority in speaking, or may teach others in an authoritative manner.... But the common people, in exhorting one another, ought not thus to exhort in an authoritative manner. There is a great deal of difference between teaching as a *father* amongst a company of children, and counseling in a *brotherly* way, as the children may kindly counsel and admonish one

---

tural rather than biblical grounds: "Most non-western societies do not embrace the egalitarian ethos and structure of church leadership put forth by the CPM paradigm." ("Wrinkling Time in the Missionary Task: A Theological Review of Church Planting Movements Methodology" (*Southwestern Journal of Theology*, 55:1, Fall 2012, 125.) Ironically, the vast majority of the over 1,900 known Church Planting and Disciple Making Movements exist among non-Western peoples. They apparently don't share Massey's objection on their behalf.

another. Those that are mere brethren ought not to assume authority in exhorting, though one may be better, and have more experience than another. Lay-men ought not to exhort as though they were the ambassadors or messengers of Christ, as ministers do; nor should they exhort, warn, and charge *in his name* (*Thoughts*, 417).

That lay-persons ought not to exhort one another as clothed with authority, is a general rule; but it cannot justly be supposed to extend to heads of families in their own families. Every Christian family is a little church, and the heads of it are its authoritative teachers and governors. Nor can it extend to schoolmasters among their scholars; and some other cases might perhaps be mentioned, that ordinary discretion will distinguish, where a man's circumstances do properly clothe him with authority, and render it fit and suitable for him to counsel and admonish others in an authoritative manner (*Thoughts*, 417).

I believe it could be useful for those involved in consideration and discussion of movements to address this issue more openly. What do we understand to be the New Testament foundations and values of leadership vis-à-vis discipleship in God's kingdom, and to what extent do we consider a strong clergy-laity distinction to be a New Testament pattern and requirement?

Extraordinary prayer has always been a hallmark and foundational element of movements, often mentioned first in lists of factors contributing to movements.[21] Edwards conveys the same perspective on the importance of earnest prayer and fasting. In fact, it could be said that Edwards laid the groundwork for subsequent generations of teaching on prayer for revival and earnest prayer for God to move powerfully. Michael McClymond notes:

> In *Humble Attempt* (1748) Edwards promoted the transatlantic "concert of prayer" in which congregations in far-flung locations united to pray for revival on the same day of the month. This work had widespread historical influence throughout the 1800s, and again, since the 1980s, reemerged as a seminal work in the international Christian prayer movement.[22]

Edwards lists prayer and fasting as the very first of all the things he strongly encourages, for those who want to see more of God's gracious work. He also calls for great zeal among leaders, if they desire to see "any thing

---

[21] David Garrison lists "Extraordinary Prayer" as the first of his 10 "Universal Elements" (*Church Planting Movements*, 172).
Samuel Kebreab describes this as the first of his seven features of Disciple Making Movements: "DMMs Depend Heavily on Prayer.... Every DMM we have the privilege of witnessing traces its origin to intense intercessory prayer and fasting...." ("Observations Over Fifteen Years of Disciple Making Movements," in *Motus Dei*, 27.)

[22] "Christian Revival and Renewal Movements," in *The Wiley Blackwell Companion to World Christianity,* First Edition, edited by Lamin Sanneh and Michael J. McClymond, 244-262. (Chichester: John Wiley & Sons, Ltd., 2016) 248.

very remarkable." He even uses the phrase "extraordinary prayers," now heard commonly among proponents of movements as "extraordinary prayer."

> *Of some particulars that concern all in general.*
> And here, the first thing I shall mention, is *fasting and prayer.* It seems to me, that the circumstances of the present work do loudly call God's people to abound in this; whether they consider their own *experience,* or the riches of God's *grace.* God has lately given them an experience of the worth of his presence, and of the blessed fruits of the effusions of his Spirit, to excite them to pray for the continuance and increase, and greater extent of such blessings (*Thoughts*, 426).
>
> So it is God's will, through his wonderful grace, that the prayers of his saints should be one great and principal means of carrying on the designs of Christ's kingdom in the world. When God has something very great to accomplish for his church, it is his will that there should precede it the extraordinary prayers of his people (*Thoughts*, 426).
>
> I should think the people of God in this land, at such a time as this is, would be in the way of their duty while doing three times as much at fasting and prayer as they do; not only, nor principally, for the pouring out of the Spirit on those towns or places where they belong; but that God would appear for his church, and, in mercy to miserable men, carry on his work

in the land, and in the world, and fulfill the things he has spoken of in his word, that his church has been so long wishing, and hoping, and waiting for (Thoughts, 426).

There is no way that Christians, in a private capacity, can do so much to promote the work of God, and advance the kingdom of Christ, as by prayer.... if they have much of the spirit of grace and supplication, in this way they may have power with Him that is infinite in power, and has the government of the whole world. A poor man in his cottage may have a blessed influence all over the world. God is, if I may so say, at the command of the prayer of faith; and in this respect is, as it were, under the power of his people; *as princes they have power with God, and prevail*" (*Thoughts*, 426).

"If the people of God at this day... would... spend more time in fasting and prayer, they would be more in the way of a blessing" (*Thoughts*, 427).
There have been frequent, plain, sensible, and immediate answers of prayer (*Thoughts*, 378).

The state of the times extremely requires a fullness of the divine spirit in ministers, and we ought to give ourselves no rest till we have obtained it. And, in order to this, I should think ministers, above all persons, ought to be much in prayer and fasting, both in secret and one with another (*Thoughts*, 424).

Two things exceeding needful in ministers, as they would do any great matters to advance the kingdom of Christ, are *zeal* and *resolution*. Their influence and power, to bring to pass great effects, is greater than can well be imagined. A man of but an ordinary capacity, will do more with them, than one of ten times the parts and learning, without them; more may be done with them in a few days, or at least weeks, than can be done without them in many years (*Thoughts*, 424).

Our misery is want of zeal and courage; for not only through want of them, does all fail that we seem to attempt, but it prevents our attempting any thing very remarkable, for the kingdom of Christ (*Thoughts*, 424).

On a closely related note, fervency of prayer has been cited as a common positive factor in movements.[23] Sam Storms highlights, in paraphrased form, the high value Edwards placed on fervency in all spiritual matters:

> THE SORT OF RELIGION or spirituality that pleases God is one that consists largely in **"vigorous and lively actings"** of the inclination and will of the soul, or **the fervent exer-**

---

[23] Steve Smith and Stan Parks: "Fervent Prayer: Perhaps it is the desperation of facing an overwhelming task in often hostile areas that drives the CPM catalysts and emerging local believers and leaders to pray more fervently than they ever have before. They pray in faith expecting God to fulfill his Word." ("T4T or DMM (DBS)? Only God Can Start a Church-Planting Movement" *Mission Frontiers,* January 01, 2015, 37.)
Kebreab uses the phrase "intense intercessory prayer and fasting...." (op. cit., 27.)

cises of the heart." God is displeased with weak, dull, and lifeless inclinations. Scripture speaks often and with divine approval of earnest and fervent affections of the soul (see Rom. 12:11; Deut. 10:12; 6:4–5; 30:6).

Spirituality is actually of little benefit to anyone if not characterized by **lively and powerful affections. Nothing is so antithetical to true religion as lukewarmness**. Consider those many biblical texts in which our relationship to God is compared to "running, wrestling or agonizing for a great prize or crown, and fighting with strong enemies that seek our lives, and warring as those that by violence take a city or kingdom" (*Storms*, 47).

Surprisingly, in light of all this, one recent critic of movements has *objected* to fervent prayer as something that should not be encouraged.[24] Different approaches

---

[24] Matt Rhodes' warns at length against the "danger" of valuing extraordinary prayer or fasting: "I don't mean to undermine prayer. It is vital, essential work. But there's a danger here if we imagine that our prayers are more effective if we pray in heroic ways." (*No Shortcut to Success*, 237).

"…it may be that we don't need to do any more than express to God, respectfully and seriously, what we hope for" (ibid. 240).

"But provided that we pray respectfully and seriously and don't give up, then we need not worry about the rest. The length of time we pray, the intensity with which we pray, the certainty we have as we pray – none of that is very important" (ibid. 242).

"Just as we should be wary of imagining that praying longer or more intensely adds power to our prayers, so we should be wary of seeing fasting as the "atomic bomb" of prayer…. There is no suggestion in Scripture that fasting makes our prayers more

to prayer (fervent with fasting vs. "respectful and serious") range much wider than discussions about movements. Yet this point seems noteworthy, since both Edwards and movement proponents have highlighted it so strongly and it has arisen as a criticism of movement characteristics.

One final comment of Edwards from "Thoughts on the Revival" seems worth noting. He strongly encourages **awareness of whatever factors tend to either hinder or aim for an increase** in the powerful move of God being observed. He encourages readers to hope God will "bless any means" of showing his glory in this move and apply "due methods, to endeavor to promote it."

> And it is a thousand pities that we should fail of that which would be so glorious, for want of being sensible of our opportunity, or being aware of those things that tend to hinder it, or taking improper courses to obtain it, or not being sensible in what way God expects we should seek it. If it should please God to bless any means for convincing the country of his hand in this work, for bringing them fully and freely to acknowledge his glorious power and

---

powerful or that it is necessary for success in ministry" (ibid. 243).

"So the amount of prayer doesn't seem overly important. What about the intensity of prayer? Must we pray with unusual intensity?" (ibid. 240). In a footnote, he cites a possible objection from James 5:17-18 (Elijah prayed "earnestly" NIV "fervently" ESV). He responds: "I do not think we can interpret Elijah's 'fervency' simply as powerful emotion," preferring to interpret it as "calm confidence" (ibid. 250).

> grace in it; and for bringing them to engage with one heart and soul, and by due methods, to endeavor to promote it, it would be a dispensation of Divine Providence that would have a most glorious aspect, happily signifying the approach of great and glorious things to the church of God, and justly causing us to hope that Christ would speedily come, to set up his kingdom of tight, holiness, peace and joy on earth, as is foretold in his word. *Amen. Even so come Lord Jesus*" (*Thoughts*, 430).

This mention of means and methods returns us to the previous discussion of methods applied in ministry. Contrary to some movement critics, who call for limiting all ministry to the methods "prescribed by the Scriptures" or those "understood, employed, and taught by the apostle Paul," proponents of movements resonate with Edwards' desire that God would "bless any means" to reveal his glory, "causing us to hope that Christ would speedily come."

Numerous means of gospel proclamation modeled by Jesus (as recorded in the Gospels) and the Apostles (as recorded in Acts) can be, and are being, fruitfully used in our day. Rather than limiting gospel proclamation to the methods explicitly "prescribed" in Scripture, it seems clear to me that Jonathan Edwards would incline toward favoring use of *all* possible means (consistent with Scripture) to proclaim the gospel to the unreached.

Conclusion

If we could invite Jonathan Edwards into our current discussions about Church Planting Movements and Disciple Making Movements, what might he say? This has been an attempt to apply relevant insights (both pro and con) from the context in which he ministered and wrote, to movements in the twenty-first century. Others might analyze and apply his perspectives differently. But it seems likely to me that on one hand, Edwards might express concerns about extensive ministry by unordained persons, and significant ministry undertaken based on subjective spiritual impressions. At the same time, he would likely recognize these movements as genuine works of God's Spirit, and would call all sincere believers to encourage these movements and participate in whatever ways they could. It seems the greater weight of his contribution would be strongly favorable toward the movements taking place in our time. I suspect Edwards would offer some words of caution to proponents of these movements, and strong words of warning to those who oppose them. Ultimately, he would call us all to look beyond his own counsel and look afresh at the Scriptures on which he built his arguments for discernment and acknowledging the marks of a true work of God's Spirit.

Books Cited

Clark, Elliot. Mission Affirmed (Wheaton, IL: Crossway, 2022)

Edwards, Jonathan. "A Treatise Concerning Religious Affections." In *The Works of Jonathan Edwards, Volume 1,* 236-343. (Carlisle, PA: The Banner of Truth Trust, 1974)

Edwards, Jonathan. "A Faithful Narrative of the Surprising Work of God in the Conversion of many hundred souls in Northampton, and the Neighbouring Towns and Villages of the County of Hampshire, in the Province of the Massachusetts-Bay in New England." In *The Works of Jonathan Edwards, Volume 1,* 346-364. (Carlisle, PA: The Banner of Truth Trust, 1974)

Edwards, Jonathan. "The Distinguishing Marks of a Work of the Spirit of God." In *The Works of Jonathan Edwards, Volume 2,* 260-277. (Carlisle, PA: The Banner of Truth Trust, 1974)

Edwards, Jonathan. "Thoughts on the Revival." In *The Works of Jonathan Edwards, Volume 1,* 366-430. (Carlisle, PA: The Banner of Truth Trust, 1974)

Farah, Warrick. *Motus Dei: The Movement of God to Disciple the Nations.* (Pasadena, CA: William Carey Publishing, 2021)
This fairly recent compendium is highly recommended for further reading, as it offers a variety of perspectives on current movements in various parts of the world.

Garrison, David. *Church Planting Movements: How God is Redeeming a Lost World.* (Arkadelphia, AR: Wigtake Resources, 2004)

Grudem, Wayne. "Gifts of the Holy Spirit," *in Systematic Theology.* (Grand Rapids, MI: Zondervan, 1994)

Grudem, Wayne. *The Gift of Prophecy in 1 Corinthians.* (Eugene, OR: Wipf and Stock, 2000)

Grudem, Wayne. *The Gift of Prophecy in the New Testament and Today.* (Wheaton, IL: Crossway, 2000)

John, Victor and Dave Coles. *Bhojpuri Breakthrough: A Movement that Keeps Multiplying* (Monument, CO: WIGTake Resources, 2019)

Larsen, Trevor, et. Al. Focus On Fruit - Case Studies and Fruitful Practices, www.focusonfruit.org

Parks, Stan and Dave Coles. *24:14 – A Testimony to All Peoples.* (Spring, Texas: 24:14, 2019)

Rhodes, Matt. *No Shortcut to Success: A Manifesto for Modern Missions* (9Marks). (Wheaton, IL: Crossway, 2021)

Sanneh, Lamin and Michael J. McClymond. "Christian Revival and Renewal Movements," in *The Wiley Blackwell Companion to World Christianity*, First Edition, (Chichester: John Wiley & Sons, Ltd., 2016)

Storms, Sam. *Signs of the Spirit: An Interpretation of Jonathan Edwards's "Religious Affections."* (Wheaton, IL: Crossway, 2007)

Vegas, Chad and Alex Kocman. *Missions by the Book: How Theology and Missions Walk Together*. (Cape Coral, FL: Founders Press, 2021)